Songs by British and American Composers

T0081806

THE DEVELOPING
Classical
Singer

BARITONE

ISBN 978-1-4950-9434-7

To access companion recorded piano accompaniments online, visit:
www.halleonard.com/mylibrary

Enter Code
4010-5725-5785-5355

DISTRIBUTED BY

HAL•LEONARD®
7777 W. BLUEMOUND RD. P.O. BOX 13819 MILWAUKEE, WI 53213

www.boosey.com
www.halleonard.com

PREFACE

The Developing Classical Singer was compiled from the rich choices in the Boosey & Hawkes catalogue, with songs in English by British and American composers. The selection of songs is for the teenage voice, or an early level collegiate singer, or an adult amateur taking voice lessons.

The songs were chosen with some specific issues in mind: vocal ranges that are not extreme, and musical challenges that are manageable for a singer at this level. Beyond art song, we have included folksong arrangements, such as those by Aaron Copland and Benjamin Britten, that are fully composed in the spirit of an art song, designed for a classical voice.

There are different compilations for each voice type: soprano, mezzo-soprano, tenor and baritone. Some cornerstone songs are in all volumes, because of their beauty and appropriateness for any voice. These include Britten's "O Waly, Waly"; Ireland's "Spring Sorrow"; Britten's realization of Purcell's "I attempt from love's sickness to fly"; Quilter's "Weep you no more"; and Vaughan Williams' "Bright is the ring of words." Beyond that, it is the editor's subjective choice about which songs work best for each voice type. Gender is certainly a factor in this, but also just the vocal sound and color of a song. Original keys of the songs were considered, but since nearly every composer of art song is not opposed to transposition, original keys were not a confining factor in which volume a song lands.

A few pedagogical reasons for assigning songs to students, though many other topics could be addressed:

Agility
I attempt from love's sickness to fly
I'll sail upon the Dog-star

Breath Support for a Long Phrase
Greensleeves
The Salley Gardens

Building an Expressive Legato Phrase
As Ever I Saw
O Waly, Waly
Simple Gifts
Spring Sorrow
Weep you no more

Expanding Vocal Range
I'll sail upon the Dog-star
It was a lover and his lass
Stopping by Woods on a Snowy Evening

Dynamic Contrasts
The Little Horses
O mistress mine
Youth and Love

Sensitively Expressing Poetry
Bright is the ring of words
Central Park at Dusk
Come away, come away, death
Fear no more the heat o' the sun
Stopping by Woods on a Snowy Evening

Building Musicianship
Morning

Personality and Storytelling
I bought me a cat
Master Kilby
Money, O!
The Vagabond
Three Poor Mariners

Baritone voices come in many varieties. Some developing baritones have faint sound in the low notes, and with that in mind, notes below C (the C below middle C) are encountered fairly infrequently in these songs in these keys, and most often are short notes when they do occur. There are plenty of songs for those voices more comfortable staying below the D above middle C. And there are some songs for those voices that naturally and easily sing higher in the range. However, the highest vocal note in this entire book is the E above middle C, which keeps it to a student singer's range.

Beyond the music, singers should learn to consider the words carefully, understanding them apart from the music, and pondering what the composer intended with the setting of the words to notes. This is the way into true personal expression, and is the real secret to becoming an artist as a performer of art song.

Richard Walters
Editor

CONTENTS

Pianists on the recordings: [1] Laura Ward, [2] Brendan Fox, [3] Richard Walters

Greensleeves

Traditional Folk Song

from *Tom Bowling and Other Song Arrangements*

original key: a minor 3rd higher

Arranged by
BENJAMIN BRITTEN

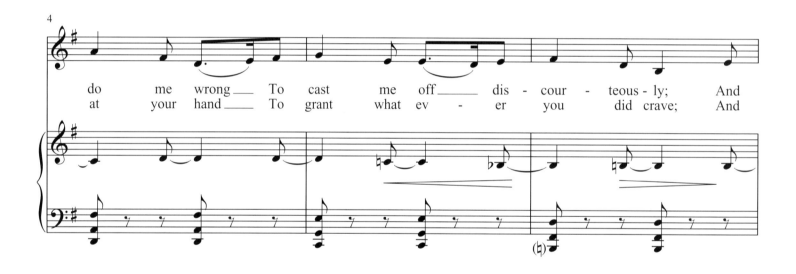

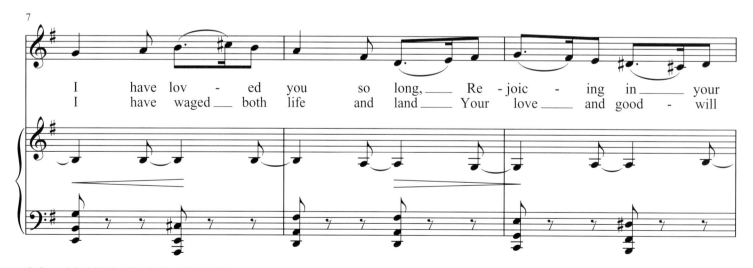

com - pa - ny.
for   to gain.   Green - sleeves _ was all   my joy, _____   Green - sleeves _ was

my de - light.   Green - sleeves was my heart   of gold, __ And who but my la - dy

dim.

Green - sleeves?

Master Kilby

from *Folksong Arrangements Volume 6: England*

original key: a major 3rd higher

*Words and Melody from
"Folk Songs for Schools"*
collected and arranged by CECIL J. SHARP

Folk Song from Somerset
Arranged for voice and guitar by
BENJAMIN BRITTEN
Transcribed for piano by
Richard Walters

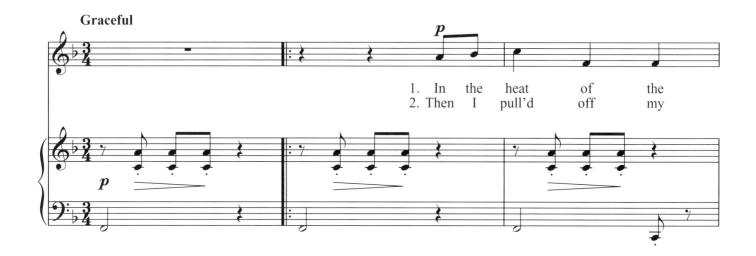

To Clytie Mundy

The Salley Gardens

Irish Tune

from *Folksong Arrangements Volume 1: British Isles*

original key: a perfect 4th higher

*Words by
W. B. YEATS

Arranged by
BENJAMIN BRITTEN

Morning

from Evening, Morning, Night
three songs from *This Way to the Tomb*
original key: a major 2nd higher

RONALD DUNCAN

BENJAMIN BRITTEN

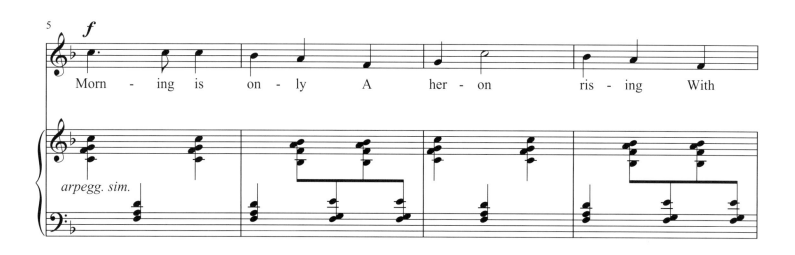

Morn - ing is on - ly A her - on ris - ing With

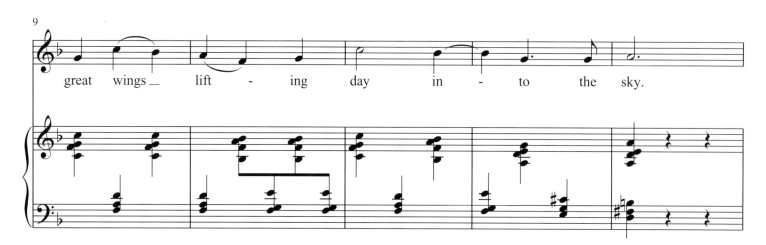

great wings lift - ing day in - to the sky.

Morn - ing is on - ly The white plumes of smoke As the

vel - vet snake Night _____ leaves the ____ green

val - ley.

O Waly, Waly

from Somerset (Cecil Sharp)*

from *Folksong Arrangements Volume 3: British Isles*

original key: a major 2nd higher

Arranged by
BENJAMIN BRITTEN

* *By permission of Messrs. Novello & Co. Ltd.*

The Little Horses
(Lullaby)

from *Old American Songs, Second Set*

original key: a major 2nd higher

Arranged by
AARON COPLAND

I bought me a cat

(Children's Song)

from *Old American Songs, First Set*

original key: a major 2nd higher

Arranged by
AARON COPLAND

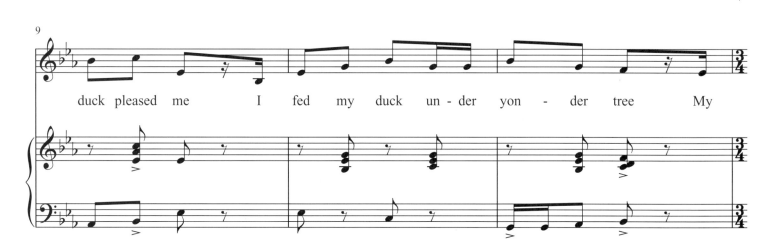

This page intentionally left blank to facilitate page turns.

Simple Gifts

(Shaker Song)

from *Old American Songs, First Set*

original key: a major 3rd higher

Arranged by
AARON COPLAND

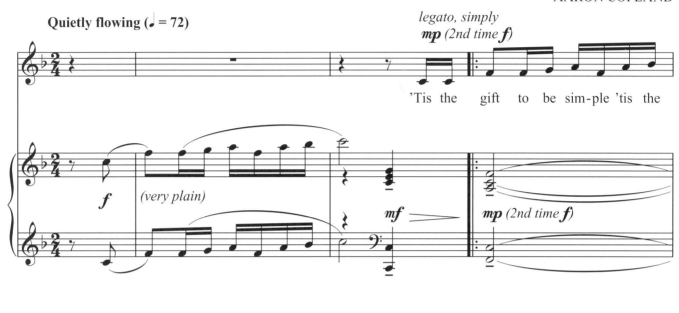

Central Park at Dusk

original key: a major 3rd higher

SARA TEASDALE*

JOHN DUKE

There is no sign of leaf or bud A hush is o - ver

eve - ry - thing. Si - lent as wom - en wait for love

The world _____ is wait - ing ___ for the spring.

For Ralph Vaughan Williams on his birthday, Oct. 12th, 1942

Come away, come away, death

from *Let Us Garlands Bring*

original key

WILLIAM SHAKESPEARE

GERALD FINZI
Op. 18, No. 1

Not a flower, _ not a flower _ sweet, _____ On my black cof - fin _____ let there be strown; _____

ritard.   **a tempo**

Not a friend, _ not a friend _____ greet _____ My poor corpse, where my bones shall _ be thrown: _____

Fear no more the heat o' the sun

from *Let Us Garlands Bring*

original key

WILLIAM SHAKESPEARE

GERALD FINZI
Op. 18, No. 3

is as the oak: The scep - tre, learn - ing, phys - ic, must

All fol-low this, and come to dust.

Fear no more the light - ning-flash, Nor the all-dread-ed

thun - der - stone; Fear not slan - der, cen - sure rash;

It was a lover and his lass

from *Let Us Garlands Bring*

original key

WILLIAM SHAKESPEARE*

GERALD FINZI
Op. 18, No. 5

*The 1623 Folio text is here collated with the version in Thomas Morley's "The First book of Ayres" 1600.

col Ped.

33
love the spring.
f dim.
37
p
Be - tween the a - cres
p
41
of the rye, With a
45
hey, and a ho, and a hey non - i - no,
mf

lov - ers love _____ the spring. _____

poco ritard.

a tempo

This car - ol they be -

gan that hour, _____ With a hey, and a

To Hester Berry

Money, O!

from *Songs of the Countryside*

original key

W.H. DAVIES

MICHAEL HEAD

Sole Selling Agent Boosey & Hawkes Music Publishers Ltd
Text used by permission of J. Cape Ltd.

Headley Down, Sept. 1928

Spring Sorrow

original key

RUPERT BROOKE

JOHN IRELAND

This Poem is reprinted from "1914 and other Poems" by Rupert Brooke,
by permission of the Literary Executor and Messrs Sidgwick and Jackson Ltd.

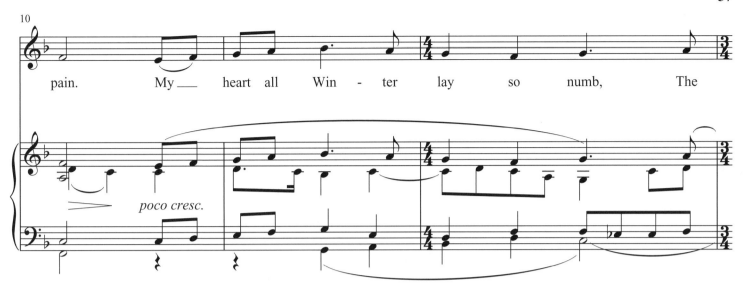

pain. My __ heart all Win - ter lay so numb, The

poco cresc.

earth so dead and frore, That I nev - er thought __ the

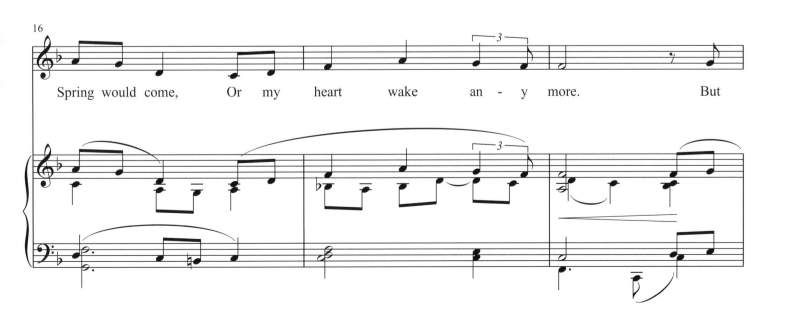

Spring would come, Or my heart wake an - y more. But

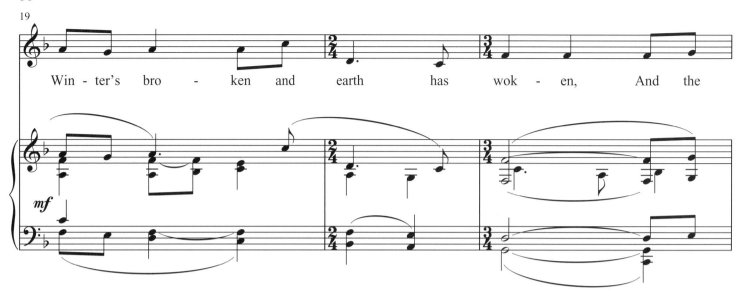

Winter's bro - ken and earth has wok - en, And the

small birds cry a - gain; And the haw - thorn hedge __ puts forth its buds And my

heart puts forth its pain. _____

April, 1918

I attempt from love's sickness to fly

from *Five Songs* (Orpheus Britannicus)

original key: a major 3rd higher

JOHN DRYDEN
and ROBERT HOWARD

HENRY PURCELL
realized by
BENJAMIN BRITTEN

For love has more pow'r and less mer- cy than fate, To make us seek ru- in, to make us seek ru- in and love those that hate. I at- tempt from love's sick- ness to fly in vain, Since I am my- self my own fe- ver, since I am my- self my own fe- ver and pain.

pp express.

dim.

(with the voice)

I'll sail upon the Dog-star

from *Seven Songs* (Orpheus Britannicus)

original key: a major 3rd higher

THOMAS D'URFEY

HENRY PURCELL
realized by
BENJAMIN BRITTEN

To Walter Creighton

O mistress mine

from *Three Shakespeare Songs, First Set*

original key: a minor 2nd higher

WILLIAM SHAKESPEARE
from *Twelfth Night*

ROGER QUILTER
Op. 6, No. 2

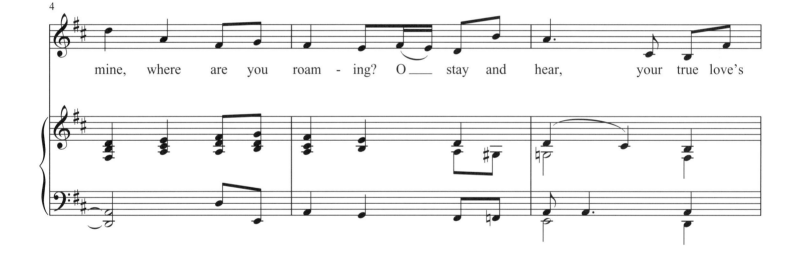

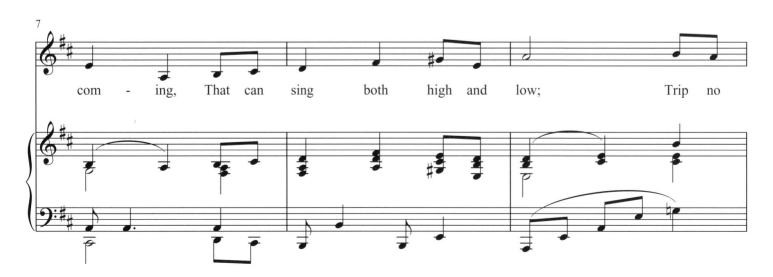

To the memory of my friend, Mrs. Cary-Elwes

Weep you no more

from *Seven Elizabethan Lyrics*

original key: a perfect 4th higher

ANONYMOUS

ROGER QUILTER
Op. 12, No. 1

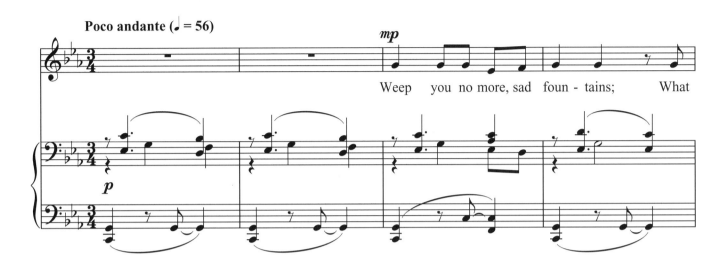

Weep you no more, sad foun - tains; What

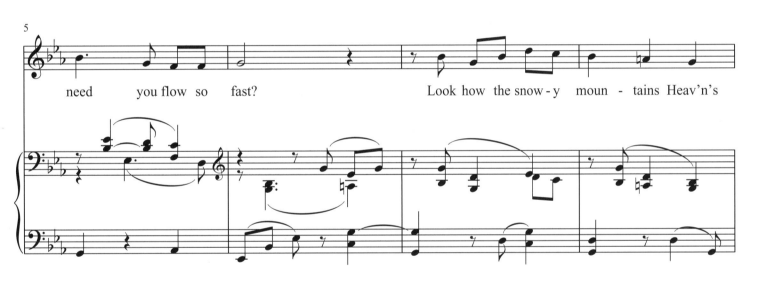

need you flow so fast? Look how the snow - y moun - tains Heav'n's

sun doth gent - ly waste! But my Sun's heav'n-ly eyes View not your

To the memory of Arnold Guy Vivian

Three Poor Mariners

from *The Arnold Book of Old Songs*

original key

ANONYMOUS

Old English Melody
arranged by
ROGER QUILTER

As Ever I Saw

original key: a minor 3rd higher

ANONYMOUS

PETER WARLOCK

Allegro

She is gen - tle and al - so wise; Of

all _____ oth - er she bear - eth the prize, That

ev - er I saw. To hear her sing, to

for my father
Stopping by Woods on a Snowy Evening
original key: a major 2nd higher

ROBERT FROST

NED ROREM

Andantino (♩ = 56)

p espr.

mp

Whose woods these are I think I know. His house is in the

vil - lage though; He will not see me stop - ping here To watch his

rit.

woods fill up with snow._____

mp

rit.

on - ly oth - er sound's the sweep Of eas - y wind and down - y flake.

The woods are love - ly, dark and deep. But I have prom - is - es to keep, And

miles to go be - fore I sleep, And miles to go be - fore I

sleep.

New York City, Thursday, 20 March 1947

Bright is the ring of words

from *Songs of Travel*

original key: a major 2nd lower

ROBERT LOUIS STEVENSON

RALPH VAUGHAN WILLIAMS

And when the west is red With the
sun - set em - bers,
The lov - er lin - gers and
sings, _____ And the maid re - mem - bers.

la melodia ben marcato.

p

pp *molto più lento*

colla voce.

pp *molto più lento*

rall.

The Vagabond

from *Songs of Travel*

original key

ROBERT LOUIS STEVENSON

RALPH VAUGHAN WILLIAMS

Allegro moderato
(alla marcia)

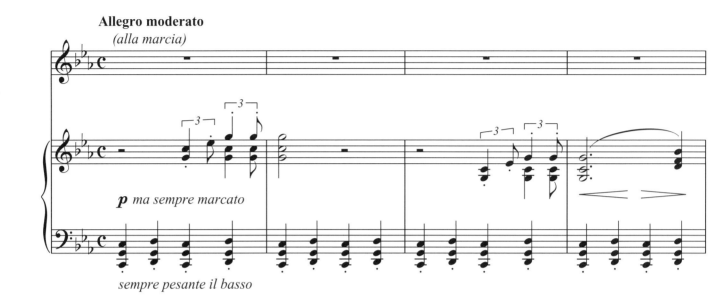

p *ma sempre marcato*

sempre pesante il basso

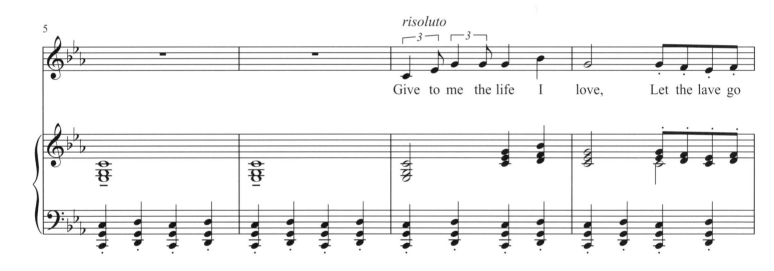

risoluto

Give to me the life I love, Let the lave go

by me, Give the jol - ly heaven a - bove, And the by-way nigh me.

o'er me; Give the face of earth a - round, And the road be - fore me.

Wealth I seek not, hope nor love, Nor a ___ friend to know

me; All I seek, the heaven a - bove, _____ And the

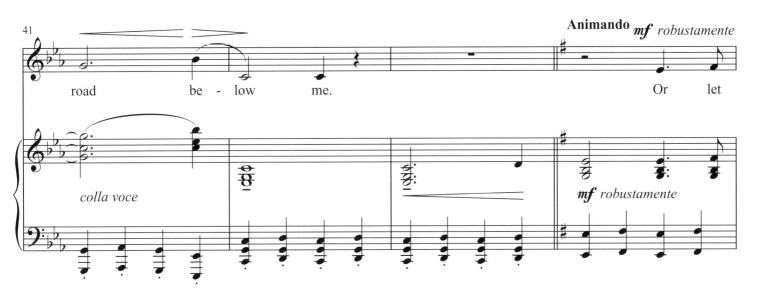

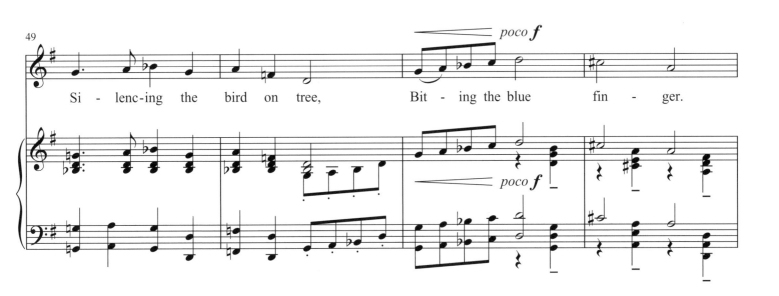

53 meno *f*

White as meal the fros-ty field— Warm the fire-side ha - ven—

meno *f*

meno *f*

57 *f ancora animando* Tempo I

Not to au - tumn will I yield, Not to win - ter

f

ff

61

e - ven!

dim.

65 **pp** *parlante*

Let the blow fall soon or late, Let what will be o'er me; Give the face of earth a -

pp *ma marcato*

Youth and Love

from *Songs of Travel*

original key

ROBERT LOUIS STEVENSON

RALPH VAUGHAN WILLIAMS